The Unclutter Angel LLC
ISBN: 9781671614277

Prayer Ideas

Being a grandparent can be one of the **greatest gifts**! What a pleasure it can be to watch our children grow and become a parent themselves. Our children need our support through many stages of life. Even as adults and parents they need our support and guidance!

One of the greatest honors we have as a parent of a grown child is becoming a grandparent! Being an active role in your grandchild's life can be very rewarding. However, our grandchildren can blessed by us even when we aren't spending one on one time with them.

Praying for our grandchildren is an honor, just like praying for our own children through the years.

What a blessing you are to your family and others that you will impact with your prayers!

Prayer Topics Ideas for:

Protection
Healing
Health
Guidance
School
Growth
Positive self-talk
Friendships
Relationships
Forgiveness
Faith
Favor
Homework
Projects
Focus
Goals

Illness
Habits
Positive self image
Awareness
Caring for others
Opportunities
Time Management
Helping others
Enjoying childhood
Transition to adulthood
Employment
Future spouse
Marriage
Future family

What else would you add?

Enjoy being a grandparent even when you can't be with your grandchildren. What a blessing to know you are praying on their behalf!

My Prayers for:

With Love,

My Special Prayers

Date: ______________________

Dear Lord,

Date: ______________________

Dear Lord,

Date: ______________________________

Dear Lord,

Date: ____________________

Dear Lord,

Date:

Dear Lord,

Date: ______________________________

Dear Lord,

Date: ______________________

Dear Lord,

Date: ______________________________

Dear Lord,

Date: ______________________

Dear Lord,

Date: ______________________________

Dear Lord,

Date: ______________________________

Dear Lord,

Date: ______________________

Dear Lord,

Date: ______________________

Dear Lord,

Date: ____________________

Dear Lord,

Date: ____________________

Dear Lord,

Date: ______________________

Dear Lord,

Date: ______________________________

Dear Lord,

Date: ______________________________

Dear Lord,

Date: ______________________

Dear Lord,

Date: ____________________

Dear Lord,

Date: ______________________________

Dear Lord,

Date: ______________________________

Dear Lord,

Date: ______________________________

Dear Lord,

Date: ______________________

Dear Lord,

Date: ______________________________

Dear Lord,

Date: ______________________

Dear Lord,

Date: ____________________

Dear Lord,

Date: ______________________

Dear Lord,

Date:

Dear Lord,

Date: ____________________

Dear Lord,

Date: ______________________________

Dear Lord,

Date: ______________________________

Dear Lord,

Date: ______________________________

Dear Lord,

Date: ______________________________

Dear Lord,

Date: ______________________________

Dear Lord,

Date:

Dear Lord,

Date: ____________________

Dear Lord,

Date: ______________________________

Dear Lord,

Date: ______________________________

Dear Lord,

Date: ______________________

Dear Lord,

Date: ______________________

Dear Lord,

Date: ______________________

Dear Lord,

Answered Prayers

SPECIAL THOUGHTS & INSIGHTS

SPECIAL THOUGHTS & INSIGHTS

SPECIAL THOUGHTS & INSIGHTS

SPECIAL THOUGHTS & INSIGHTS

SPECIAL THOUGHTS & INSIGHTS

SPECIAL THOUGHTS & INSIGHTS

SPECIAL THOUGHTS & INSIGHTS

Made in the USA
Columbia, SC
19 June 2025

59604369R00070